BAD TIMING

SOUTH AMERICA (MIS)ADVENTURES 2020

Copyright © 2020 by Jane N. Hughes

All rights reserved. No part or portion of this book may be reproduced or used in any manner without prior written permission of the copyright owner except for the use of quotations in a book review as per the Australian Copyright Act 1968

Published by
Jane N. Hughes
Melbourne, Victoria

ISBN: 978-0-6488978-0-4

Edited by Anne Schmitt & Christopher Ringrose
Cover photo by Jane N. Hughes
Cover design by Jane N. Hughes & Chloe Watson
Interior design by Chloe Watson

Disclaimer

This memoir reflects my own personal recollection of experiences during a South American Trip in 2020. The views are of what happened at the time and is not intended to hurt or harm anybody. I regret any unintentional harm resulting from the publishing of Bad Timing South America (Mis)adventures 2020. Some names have been changed to protect privacy.

BAD TIMING

SOUTH AMERICA (MIS)ADVENTURES 2020

JANE N. HUGHES

In loving memory of my mother
Penninah Wangui Ndungu.

And a very special dedication to my husband
Robert and our lovely children Brian and
Alexandria Hughes, for walking through this
journey with me.

The Dream

I've always been a dreamer. Even as a village girl in Kenya, I felt different from my peers and the idea of living what society thought of as a 'normal' life never appealed to me. Even though I cared about the people in my community when I was young, I didn't pay much attention to what they thought of me. I focussed, instead, on what I thought was good for me – the things that would help me develop as a person. As a young person my dream was just to travel; one's dreams change as one grows older, and my adult thoughts centred on a visit to Antarctica: a region different from all others, to which few people travel. In my imagination Antarctica figured as a sublime, isolated place –somewhere I wanted so much to be. But expensive! How could I afford such a trip? However, I never allowed my dream to die and kept hoping that one day I would be able to achieve it. The 'Antarctica Idea' sat at the back of my mind until the right time came, when I finally had opportunity to make it a reality. Excitement and expectations started taking shape; in a few months' time and after a few months 'going to Antarctica' was to become a reality. Nothing could stop this dream from happening.

By now we were living a suburban life in Australia, after years of working and travelling in Africa and the Pacific. In the middle of 2018, my husband Robert and I were discussing what present I wanted for my 50th birthday – this was two years before the big day. I was so excited, and my immediate response to his question was that I had always wanted to visit Antarctica, and that since I'm not a fan of big parties, that was the only thing which could make turning 50 a source of satisfaction. I was shocked and surprised when he confided in me that he, too, had always yearned to visit Antarctica, but had never thought of communicating his dream to me. Robert had thought that I wouldn't be receptive to an Antarctic trip because of the cost involved. How wrong he was! With both of us now focused on Antarctica and on the same page, we agreed that in order to provide me with a fancy birthday present we needed to start planning and organising for this trip, which lay eighteen months ahead.

Overwhelmed by the great news, I promised him I would follow it up with the travel agencies and become the world's expert about all the tours offered to Antarctica – and South America, too. We wanted to push on even further after the Antarctica expedition, since it was going to be a 'once in a lifetime' trip. I like being organised and so I jumped straight onto the computer checking what other tours this part of the world had to offer. What struck me most was how expensive these tours were. There was no way one could afford them without having very well-planned ideas for how to pay for the trip. I visited a Flight Centre office near us and got all the booklets covering Antarctica and South America. I also got in touch with different tour companies for quotes on the ones we had chosen and others we might undertake. After receiving a few emails from different travel agencies, I concluded that there was no way we could afford this trip. Instead we decided to forget about Antarctic tour companies, and organise a tour ourselves. I took the initiative of doing all the organising and collaborating with tour companies in South America.

One month after our decision to make an independent trip, I began to search for comments from other people who had undertaken this approach, to understand what I had to do and whom I could contact to find out more information.

Planning

Self-education: South American Geography, Spanish Language

I studied geography as one of my compulsory High School subjects, but it never interested me much. I thought that I had no chance of visiting the places I was learning about. But now I needed to learn more about South America, as I had no clue what it might offer us as travellers – all my research had been focused on Antarctica. I therefore put a lot of effort into learning about each individual South American country and its appeal for us. Three countries in particular – Argentina, Peru and Bolivia – had a lot of exciting tourist sites, and detailed knowledge of these places would make organising the trip easier and give us a better idea of what to do when we arrived.

The most widely-spoken language in South America is Spanish. And neither of us could speak Spanish; this was going to be a challenge! I enrolled on a 'learning Spanish' app online. Every day as I travelled to work in the train, I would listen to it, and write sentences as the app instructed. I visited a language school, where they instructed me to buy basic language books, but I gradually realised how time-consuming and expensive it was to study Spanish, so began to lose interest. I do speak a number of other languages – the ability to learn one another more was not a big issue; but I realised that I learn better from listening to people rather than reading textbooks. After six months or so I was only practising occasionally, so I took a break from Spanish, promising myself I'd go back to the app to remind myself of the basics before the trip itself.

The Travel Savings Account

Travelling does require money and the first step to turning our dream into reality was to set some money aside. To separate our daily living expenses from this new initiative, I opened a new bank account solely for travel savings (the internet is a great tool in organising such things). I set it up so that some money went automatically to the travel account every fortnight, and I did not touch or look at the account until I was confident it had accumulated reassuring amount of money. Robert trusts me to handle our money and has never queried me, since he knows I am a good financial manager. After four to five months, I felt in a position to make serious enquiries about different tours; if we were happy with what they were offering we could make a down payment without any hassles. The whole trip was going to cost approximately USD 23,000 with USD 11,200 going to the Antarctica expedition alone, the rest covering other tours, accommodation, food and flights.

Each week I would look at different Antarctica cruise ships: what they offered, how they treated their customers and what was required from them.

I also compared and contrasted the different tours I had discovered, until we finally settled on a small cruise ship which takes around eighty-eight people – not very flash, but it had received very good reviews about how they conducted their business. One of the main reasons we settled on a small ship was the intimate tours these small ships offered, in comparison to the big ships that carried more than a hundred tourists at a time. According to the laws governing Antarctica, only a hundred tourists are permitted to disembark at one time, and we didn't want to miss out on a thing.

The ship operated as the Southern Expeditions Cruise and it had initially been a research vessel. I contacted Southern Expeditions Cruise to find out what we had to do to be their customers and experience Antarctica. Their services and communication were excellent, and I could not fault anything. They clearly laid out that we had to put down ten percent of the total cost as a deposit and make the last payment three months before the start of the cruise. Robert was happy with this arrangement and we were both excited and began to 'count down' to our departure, even though it lay some months down the track.

When it was time for the deposit to be paid there was enough in the account to pay it off; it was a great feeling not having to take a loan for the trip, and we felt a burden lift off our shoulders. The funds in the account had gone down again but we continued to save as we went on with our lives. Months went by quickly and soon we had enough information on the other phase of our trip – a tour of South America. We settled on visiting Iguazu Falls, the Amazon Jungle, Cusco and Machu Picchu in Peru, before finishing at the Salar de Uyuni, the Salt Flats in Bolivia. Easier said than done – these destinations are actually huge distances from one another and until I researched them, I never realised that one would have to travel either by air or by bus (trains are very limited in most places). The buses take longer and are not safe in some places; nor did we have enough time off work to travel everywhere by road. We decided that flying was the only way we could get from one place to another, save time and manage the tour within our timeframe. So, there were four components of this trip. The first one was the Antarctic cruise ship, the second involved flights from one place to another, the third was organising accommodation and the fourth the actual site visits. We had enough time remaining to put all these components together and look forward to a pleasant and fulfilling trip.

We decided to pay for the flights, and to organise our five weeks of travel. We could fit everything we wanted to do and see within that time frame. From my research I had realised we couldn't rely solely on the flight timetables provided by airlines in South America. We had to allow enough time so that if flights were cancelled or postponed, we could be flexible and adjust our timings as we went along. All we needed to do was allow one day after every flight booking to facilitate eventualities. As they say, 'No hurry in South America'! Punctuality is not always a major factor, and South American businesses are no exception to this rule. Overall, some twelve flights were needed to cover our itinerary.

As I set about booking the tours, I picked up a lot of skills and knowledge along the way. One thing struck me in particular as I dealt with all these online flight booking agencies: there is a lot of competition for sales and appealing deals are offered which can be hard to resist. However, I did counter-check ticket prices directly with the airlines and even though I made two mistakes in booking with online agencies, I decided to book all our flights directly with the airlines concerned. The prices were no different and some were in fact cheaper than what the online agencies were offering.

The next step was to ensure that we had accommodation in each place we landed. As much as I now wanted to avoid online booking agencies, I found that in some cases there were no direct connections to the accommodation; there was no choice but to use the online agencies or risk just turning up and looking for somewhere to stay. So I went ahead and booked all our accommodation through online agencies. One benefit these agencies offered was that you did not have to pay for accommodation up front. There was also the advantage of being able to make a cancellation, provided you did so within the stipulated time frame. This was to enable us to make certain decisions as time went by.

Once we had booked these essentials, other important things remained: transport to the site entrances, plus the entrance fees. We had decided to take a taxi from Cusco to Ollantaytambo in South Peru, and see different sites along the way, followed by a train to Agua Calientes so that we could enter Machu Picchu, high in the Andes. The tickets were bought and secured online and the only thing remaining was to pick them up when we arrived in Cusco. The same applied to Machu Picchu entrance tickets. The Bolivia Salt Flats tour was left to be booked at Uyuni (most discussion sites on the internet encouraged one to do this). We were all set to go! We just had to wait for the date of departure to arrive.

There was enough money left in the travel account for the bookings and tours we had arranged. Our dream was approaching; all we had to do was wait for the take-off of our big South American trip. The remaining money in the account would pay for our accommodation and leave enough for food and incidentals. Looking back, I am very proud of our saving capacity, and our determination to reach our goals and objectives.

COVID-19 Emerges

Three months before the trip, a virus broke out in Wuhan, China. The media were circulating news about how the virus was killing many residents of this city. This virus was eventually to be formally labelled COVID–19. There was much confusion about how the illness was contracted, but the concern was that it was a respiratory disease contracted through droplets. The disease seemed to take a particular toll on the elderly, even though some young people had got it and succumbed. There was not much initial concern in Australia as we had no cases to start with in December 2019 and January 2020. Our trip was scheduled to commence on the 11th March 2020. As time progressed, more Corona virus cases were reported, continuing to increase beyond China to other countries. Australia was not immune, as we have a lot of international students coming to study from overseas, including China. The government took the initial preventative measures by isolating all those who travelled back to Australia from China; they were sent into quarantine on Christmas Island for fourteen days. If they were clear of the virus after this period, without any symptoms of COVID-19, they were released into the community. While the number of cases continued to increase in other countries, Australia had very few and there was no alarm put out by the government suggesting that one should not travel overseas. Therefore, our plans remained in place until such time as the government provided 'no travel' advice.

There was nothing but Corona virus on the media; every television or radio channel one listened to was talking about the COVID–19 and the toll it was taking in different countries. Wuhan was put into lock down: nobody could go in and out of the place and people were confined to their houses. Here in Australia we thought we were still lucky to be able to carry on with our lives and activities as usual. There were no alarms in place, and nobody would ever have thought that we were going to be seriously affected. Our trip was approaching, and we bought everything required for our journey. We also visited the bank to turn our travel savings account into a debit card account so we could use it overseas without any problems. Having done all this and being ready to travel, we were just waiting for the great day to arrive. There was no government warning that we should not travel, and the departure day was close.

Outward Bound: Our Trip Is Here

Our trip commenced on the 11th of March 2020; our plan was to be in South America when my birthday came around. Our first excitement lay in the anticipation of the Antarctica cruise ship and experiencing that part of the world. On arrival at Tullamarine Airport Melbourne, we became aware that there were very few people on the concourse. The process was smooth as silk and we proceeded to the waiting area where we found more people flying to New Zealand. Our flight was delayed by one hour then we left from Melbourne through to Auckland. We had a three hour stop-over there before boarding for Buenos Aires, twelve hours away. After we landed in Buenos Aires and had disembarked, we were going through to migration when a young man approached me and warned me that my bag was partly open. I'd forgotten that I was in a different part of the world, where I had to watch everything I owned! Some websites recommended putting padlocks on your backpack and wearing the bag at the front rather than putting it on your back. I thanked the guy, closed my bag and proceeded to the migration desk.

We were cleared quickly and headed off to look for our personal taxi waiting to pick us up. We were met by a lady with our names on a board. In my limited Spanish, I asked her where I could find a local sim card for the phone, and she directed me to the first floor. I left Robert and the bags with the taxi lady while I went to search for a phone sim card. At the telephone office, I presented my passport for registration but unfortunately the system went down when we were half-way through the registration. One of the things I learned when travelling was to avoid using my usual mobile phone, as the telephone companies in Australia charge ridiculous amount of money in 'roaming tariffs', and if you are money-conscious like myself you will be shocked at the money you end up paying if you made the mistake of using your usual phone. Disappointed, I left the office to re-join Robert, and we took our taxi to the hostel.

Our taxi driver turned out to be male; the lady had disappeared. Apparently, it had been raining the whole week before our arrival; the roads were extremely wet and we were thinking we could not have picked a worse time to visit Buenos Aires: as the rain might limit a lot of our planned activities. The driver drove like crazy! He hit 140 kilometres per hour on wet roads. I was holding my hand on my stomach, feeling sick and thinking we might have an accident before we even got to see the city. The taxi driver did not speak a word of English and between the two of us, I was the only one with a little Spanish. I decided to try out my limited vocabulary and ask whether the driver could slow down a little bit, and to break the ice. Once I started to speak Spanish the driver seemed more at ease and more pleasant. Even though there was still a language barrier, the journey to the hostel was a bit better from that point on. The roads of Buenos Aires are wide and well maintained, and the traffic seems to work in a kind of organised chaos.

It took an hour to get to our hostel. We had no Argentinian pesos at this point. I asked Robert whether he had managed to change some money while I went for the sim card but he said that he had been advised not to exchange money at the airport by the taxi lady who met us. However, she hadn't given him any alternative! While I understand that exchange rates at the airport might be crazy, it would have made sense to change just a little bit of money to have some cash with us. Otherwise, we were at risk of being ripped off and not being able to pay for goods if shops and vendors did not accept a credit card. We now found ourselves with no sim card and no money! What a great start to be in a foreign country. Anyway, we did not dwell on the money issue and focussed instead on checking into the hostel. We found a young, pleasant man at reception who went out of his way to provide us with any support we required to make us comfortable. I noticed that they also sold sim cards; we seriously needed to buy one. However, it was the same story as at the airport; the system was down. However, the hostel did have an internet connection. The wi-fi was a saviour to us, enabling us to connect to WhatsApp and communicate with family and friends. The only problem was that this form of communication was limited to the hostel premises or other Wi-Fi-enabled sites. Once we were out and about, the service ceased.

Our room was on the third floor and the lift was working at the time we arrived. We were given a quick orientation of the place and went straight to our room. Our hostel was in San Telmo province, pretty safe – but not safe enough to walk out at night. Argentina had been in recession for four years, as we learned from the local people. People have no money and they are only allowed to withdraw 5,000 pesos per day, which is equivalent to a hundred Australian dollars. We had our travel cards ready for use and some American dollars to enable us to purchase and pay for things we required. Since we had arrived at the hostel in the evening, we did not want to venture far from there, but we needed to familiarise ourselves with the environment. We also needed dinner but had no idea where we could get a meal. We asked the receptionist and he was happy to recommend a restaurant not far from the hostel. We decided to venture out to it, and indeed we felt welcomed there; with my limited Spanish I asked for the menu. The waiter was prepared for non-Spanish speakers and at this point produced his phone which contained photos and an explanation of the meals.

The Argentinians have a bread and dip entrée which is quite filling, followed by main courses of tender meats, chips and salad very large servings. We paid in American dollars before returning to our hostel. As we were going in, we met a young woman who was also looking for somewhere to eat, so we recommended our restaurant to her. The lift was out of action when we got back (some unfortunate travellers were stuck inside it) so up the three floors of stairs we went.

12th March 2020: Buenos Aires

We woke up early, excited to discover Buenos Aires, and spent an hour or so highlighting the map with areas we would like to visit. We went down for breakfast at the hostel, then tried again to get a local sim card at Reception, but nothing had changed. The system was still down, and nobody seemed to care about it. Today, it seemed like a huge effort for the receptionist to help us, which was disappointing. At least he knew where a bank with an ATM might be. We went down three blocks, dodging the dog droppings on the footpath, and joined the two-person queue at the ATM. When it was our turn, we went through all the bank process of withdrawing money, but no money was issued. By now there were five people behind us in the queue and we tried to ask why the money was not being issued. The first person was a young lady and it was like talking to a tree. She had her earphones in and did not even bother checking what was happening; she stood like a statue. Another man just kept yelling in Spanish saying that the bank would not issue money because we were not its customers. Meanwhile another older lady in the queue offered to help us by trying again and we went through the same process without any success. We left the bank with no money and went back to the hostel.

We reviewed the map about areas we wanted to visit that day and asked whether it was safe to walk to La Boca, listed as one of the most colourful districts in *Buenos Aires*, since it was within walking distance of where we were staying. The response to our question was that it was unsafe to go to La Boca without a local resident who knew the area well. With our plans thrown into doubt, we were confused and not sure what else we could do as tourists. The hostel informed us that they organise tours to different locations each day and today they were visiting the main Buenos Aires historical sites. So we decided to take up this offer. To enable us to visit these places we needed travel cards for the buses which were provided by the hostel. The cards had a little bit of credit on them, but we had to give them back with the same credit when we finished up with them.

Buenos Aires is such a big city, with a train system

as well as buses. As a group of six people from the same hostel we embarked on a long day through Buenos Aires, stopping in a shop to top up on the travel cards as we went. We walked two blocks down and boarded a bus to the main sites. In our group was a couple who were doing a tour of South America before they went back to England; they had spent some time working in Australia. There was also an Argentinian lady who lived down in the south of the country and was visiting Buenos Aires. And in addition, the lady we met the day before, who had asked us about dinner. We got to know each other and found she was called Nesa, from Switzerland, and that she had embarked on a six-month tour, starting in South America and hoping to end in Australia. The city of Buenos Aires is known to have the highest crime rate in the world, and the lady who ran the tour warned us to look after our personal belongings and not to carry anything which would attract attention. There are very few black people in Argentina and from my research I had learned that the country had killed their entire black population in the 1800s as they wanted their population to be a purely white. However, as a black person one does not feel threatened, due to one's colour. As an African Australian, I felt at ease and interacted with people without any issues. While in South America I decided to put my Spanish to use even though it was not perfect; I could understand some of the things going on, and I could communicate a little bit.

Our first visit was to San Miguel province, where we saw different historical icons. Our first shock of the day came when we were just walking along the road right before the Federal Police Station, where police were standing at the side of the road. On the opposite side, a middle-aged man got out of his vehicle, stood against his car, removed his penis and scrotum from his trousers and did a massive urination right in front of the police. People just glanced across and manifested little reaction to the driver. Nor did the police pay any attention to him. He finished his business, went back to his vehicle and drove off as if nothing had happened.

We took a walk between the jacaranda trees which was amazing and refreshing. We also visited Floralis Generica, a metal flower sculpture in the Plaza de las Naciones Unidas, designed by Argentinian architect Eduardo Catalano. Its flower petals are supposed to open in the morning and close in the evening using solar energy, but unfortunately not enough money has been allocated to maintain this movement and it is now just a static sculpture. However, it still attracts a lot of tourists due to its impressive size. While I enjoy seeing the historical and iconic things on my travels, people are just as interesting to me and I am a great observer of everyday life happening around me all the time.

We passed the University of Buenos Aires, a huge building with nothing much to offer in terms of attraction. It was just another learning institute. We went through the park, where people were relaxing in just the same way you can find in any part of the world. However, as we were passing the drinking tap, we observed a couple taking a full shower in the water stream – the woman giving her friend a proper clean up. I wasn't sure whether they were homeless (as there were few people on Buenos Aires streets who were begging), but I couldn't help but find it very unhygienic to use the same water supplied in the park for everyone else to use for drinking purposes. The couple seemed unbothered by the people passing by. A few steps further down the park, another couple were almost having sex in the open! The police were walking by just next to this couple and did not seem to be even a little bit concerned. Our guide just told us to keep going. We could not take photos for security reasons so the only option we had was to use our phones as a backup camera. As we walked along the streets and parks there were lots of activities going on; the elderly, in particular, were doing all sorts of exercises; plus, there were people roller skating, running, walking, and doing yoga. Others were having weddings or just enjoying what nature has to offer. It doesn't matter which part of the world you live in. We are all the same.

    We next arrived at the Recoleta, the great cemetery and museum where famous and powerful Argentinians were laid to rest. No fee is charged at the entrance and one is permitted to walk around taking photos without any issues. This cemetery contains the remains of leaders from the 18th and 19th centuries, and some coffins are still visible. Eva Peron has an elaborate tomb here. As a massive number of people visit this museum, one needs to ensure that cameras and personal effects are well secured; wearing the backpack in front is the best strategy, I soon realised. One just needs to look after one's own personal property. During our walk we got to talk to Nesa the Swiss lady – a nice person to have a wider discussion with. She confided in us that she hated eating alone in restaurants and therefore had not eaten proper food for a number of days. Of course, we asked her to join us for dinner that night so that we could provide her with the companionship she enjoyed. She also shared with us a lot about her travels in South America so far, and how different countries treated tourists. As we had spent this whole day without eating and drinking a thing, we decided to spoil ourselves with a nice ice-cream to round the day off. The tour group dispersed, and our tour guide, Nesa, Robert and I took a bus to an ice cream parlour. Our ice-cream was lovely, and the tour guide left for home. Nesa, Robert and I decided to walk back to our hostel which took a long time, especially as we were already tired and exhausted. On that day we walked eighteen kilometres! We agreed that we would have a good shower, a rest, then the three of us would go for dinner.

After a nice two hours rest, we met at the hostel foyer and brainstormed which restaurant we could visit to try a typical Argentinian meal. We all settled on La Brigada, one of the best-known restaurants, where they provided authentic high-quality Argentinian food. (Nesa is a vegetarian, but on this evening, she decided to have some meat and just enjoy a different kind of meal). The restaurant turned out to be three blocks down the street from our hostel; the vibe was good and we secured a table for three people. The service was excellent, and the staff were jovial; it was the perfect place to relax after such a big day of walking. The variety of food on the menu was mind-blowing. We settled on meat, vegetables and mashed sweet potatoes, which seem to be a delicacy in this part of the world, and shared a bottle of wine between the three of us. We had such a beautiful dinner with Nesa, who we got to know a little bit better. After two hours in the restaurant we walked back to our hostel for the night. It had been such a big day that had ended up with a nice meal and pleasant company. This was our last night in Buenos Aires, as we were travelling south to Ushuaia on the Tierra del Fuego archipelago the next day.

13th March 2020

We woke up early ready to travel to Ushuaia, from where we were going to take the cruise ship to Antarctica. While we were having our usual breakfast, Nesa arrived to say goodbye; we wished her well for her trip to Australia. Until one lives in Australia one cannot comprehend how big the country is, and Nesa was no different – she had no idea. Her plan was to take a combi van to Broome, then Esperance – both beautiful places to visit but the distances from one place to another are huge. We therefore took time to educate Nesa that Australia was such a big country and she would be driving for a long time without seeing anybody on the roads, maybe for days. We also had fun educating Nesa on how to be an Aussie and learning how to pronounce words such as 'nice' (noice) and good on you (good onya) and she found all these things fascinating. She was looking forward to visiting Australia and enjoying her holiday. After this morning interaction, Nesa was leaving to visit La Boca on one of the tours organised by the hostel, and we were heading to the airport for our flight to Ushuaia. I was disappointed that I never got a chance to visit La Boca, which everyone says is a very colourful lively district of the city, where they dance the tango. It's also known for producing the country's greatest soccer players. But our trip had to continue.

    We asked the receptionist to call a taxi. Seriously, it was like talking to a stone. His attitude was that of a spoilt teenage and I wondered why on earth they kept him at the front office to cater to tourists. I also gave up on purchasing a sim card from this hostel.

Finally, the taxi driver arrived, and we were off to the airport. On arrival he said we owed him 70 US dollars for a fifteen-minute drive. Robert and I protested in our broken Spanish, and he eventually charged 50 dollars. Normally it would have cost 25 dollars, but you live and learn. We presented our ticket to the desk at the airline we had booked with through one of the online agencies. When I made the booking, I noted that one piece of luggage was allowed, and had assumed this was the checked-in luggage as the ticket never mentioned hand baggage at all. The clerk at the counter was blunt and completely rude, and said the ticket had been bought a year ago and luggage was not paid for.

Robert tried to make him point out on our ticket where the luggage was indicated. Despite the fact that he could not find anything concerning the luggage, he pushed us to the pay office and never paid attention to any of our concerns. Since I was the one who had made the booking, my heart was racing, thinking maybe all our other tickets were the same. But after checking them out I realised I had purchased the other tickets directly from the airlines themselves, and that they allowed 23 kilos of luggage, plus hand baggage. We went to the pay office, where this time the lady was extremely helpful, explaining that if she had to charge for the luggage direct from her computer the fee was going to be high, but if we logged in to the internet ourselves it could save us money. At the airport, the wi-fi worked fine; we logged in and got the luggage paid for within five minutes. It did not cost much, but it was still annoying to have to do it when we thought everything was already paid for. While at the airport we managed to purchase the long-awaited local sim card and were all ready for our next leg of travel.

Ushuaia

We left for Ushuaia from Buenos Aires, and for the first time in my flying history I experienced cabin crew members who had absolutely no interest in their customers. This was so unusual and unprofessional. The crew spent their time chatting to each other and never cared one jot about the comfort of their clients. We sat in our allocated seats and there came a message that due to COVID-19 the airline would not be providing any refreshments during the flight. Even after landing there was not a single goodbye from the cabin staff. On landing in Ushuaia, the sights were amazing. We had seen mountains and lakes from the sky, and the sights from the ground were equally lovely. We arrived in Ushuaia at round 15.00 hours and called our accommodation to find out whether they were going to send a taxi for us. The lady who answered, Noni, spoke no English, and hence my broken Spanish came in handy, even though sometimes it was hard to understand what she was saying. She said we were to take a taxi to her place, and it would cost approximately 20 Australian dollars. The taxi drivers always try to charge a little bit more if you are not aware of the prices, but once I pointed out the suggested amount, the guy had no issues and he drove us to our bed and breakfast, Laguna Esmeralda. We found Noni waiting for us – the place was a three-storey house, not particularly big, but good enough for us.

We paid for our accommodation and Noni took us to our room. The third floor had a kitchen where we could cook, and breakfast was served there. The toilet and bathroom were shared between two rooms. One thing which certainly surprised me was using the toilet without putting toilet paper into the toilet itself; after using the toilet paper one dropped it in a bucket. Well, my background is Kenyan, and when I was young, we used an outside toilet where we dropped our paper in the hole, therefore I found this new routine very weird. But as they say, 'when in Rome you do as Romans do'. Or as the Ushuaians do. (I later found out that the sewage pipes are so narrow they cannot take toilet paper through the system, hence toilet paper has to be separated from the main waste). Anyway, we went out to the town centre and saw what the small settlement had to offer. We asked our host where the best place to have a nice meal might be, and her recommendation was great.

Noni had suggested a small place called Bodegon Fueguino, and the services and food there were amazing. We left the place ready for bed but when we arrived back at the accommodation Robert realised that he lost his keys. Catastrophe. We looked for them everywhere, without success. I tried to call the restaurant to see whether they had fallen out of his pocket while he was paying the bill, but my Spanish was not good enough for us to communicate that. He decided to go and look for it himself. Success and celebration! The keys were on the floor. Relived and able to get into our accommodation, we had a good night's sleep, ready for the next day's adventure.

14th March 2020

On our second day in Ushuaia we decided to visit the cruise company just to find out whether the planned Antarctic cruise was still on. Initially I had tried to call them, but nobody answered the phones. We were becoming anxious. In early March, Europe was struggling with coronavirus and things were starting to change – and fast! We never thought we would be affected by COVID-19, since Australia had very few cases. Here in Argentina, fewer than ten cases had been reported, and businesses were running as usual. It took us 30 minutes to find Southern Expeditions Cruise, as their address was far from obvious on Google maps. We asked a number of people, none of whom had any idea about this company, and I began to have the niggling thought that I might have been scammed. However, I kept this thought to myself and did not communicate it to Robert. After walking up and down searching for the address, I tried to call them one more time and finally, somebody answered their phone. I felt such relief, since I had nearly given up. The receptionist told us where they were based, and we finally found a lady who welcomed us and confirmed that they were operating as usual. She said the only people who were not allowed on the cruise were those from Europe and China who were affected by the virus. We confirmed that the cruise was going ahead on the 17th March at 16.00 hours. The company also informed us that they took temperatures before boarding and we had to fill in a declaration form confirming that we had not had contact with anyone who was affected by COVID-19. As you can imagine, having confirmed our cruise Robert and I left a happy couple.

Next was shopping for dinner, so we stopped at the supermarket, chose some food then waited at the till. The cashiers did not acknowledge that we were waiting and ignored our presence. I was reorganising the goods and Robert was going to pay for them. The cashier, however, was busy chatting to her mate. When it was time for Robert to pay, he presented his Visa card for processing. The cashier said she needed a passport for the goods to be paid for, to ensure the card belonged to Robert. She also mumbled that the card might not belong to him. Of course, we had left our passports back at the accommodation and could not pay for our groceries. I unpacked all the goods I had put in our shopping bag, put them back on their counters and left disappointed. There were absolutely no customer care concerns, and the people who were dealing with us did not care about our plight in the slightest. I simply could not understand this poor attitude, as the country's economy was already in a terrible state. And things were just about to get worse once the corona virus started to affect everybody. Fortunately, there was another supermarket forty meters away from our accommodation and we decided to give it a go. We bought our groceries from there without a hitch and left for home; no passports needed to buy groceries there!

Back at the accommodation we met a young couple from Germany, who told us that they were stuck in the town, since the Argentinian government had cancelled all flights in and out of Europe. They were considering driving back to Buenos Aires from Ushuaia then trying for a flight to Brazil which was still open to incoming and outgoing European flights. After this interaction, in the back of my mind, I started wondering whether the Antarctica trip was ever going to go ahead as promised. As there was no communication from the cruise company about cancellation, we lived in hope, waiting for the day to arrive.

Ushuaia is not a big town. However, it extends across the foothills of the mountains, and offers other tours like hiking and visits to historical sites.

We spent the afternoon hiking the Martial Glacier – it is a long and uneven walk of about 7.1 kilometres, and I found it very steep; it was seriously hard work to get to the glacier. Some of the trails were very unsafe and with the slightest mis-step one would be rolling down the mountain. In this part of the world safety is not a priority it seems, and the government/rangers have not indicated or marked areas of danger. After two-and-a-half hours I managed to reach the glacier, exhausted and cold. From the top of the mountain the view of Ushuaia was very pretty and amazing. Robert did not manage to get to the top, as it was challenging for him; also, he is afraid of heights. He flagged down a young man who was also doing the hike and asked him to pass a message to me that he was not going to make it to the top, and that he had decided to start back down the trail. I was way ahead of Robert, and I am glad he made the right decision to not come all the way up, as it was very difficult. The descent was equally difficult, if not more so – the steep gradient and the pressure on one's knees were hard to handle. I am glad I did this hike, but I would never consider doing it again. We cooked our dinner and we were excited to see what the next day had to offer.

15th March 2020

A long-time friend of Robert, Alan, was joining us for the Antarctica trip and was arriving in Ushuaia around midday. We had morning breakfast and just chilled waiting for the time to pass by until pick-up at the airport. I had been using my Spanish more often here, as our host did not speak a word of English. I asked her to call a taxi for us, to pick us up from the airport in an hour and a half. The airport was not far from our accommodation, so we walked there in 55 minutes. Our walk was also our exercise for the day, even though our leg muscles were tight from the previous day's glacier trek. We did not wait for long before the taxi man yelled my name, so we only needed to wait for Alan. He came through customs, and we headed off to the accommodation. He paid for his accommodation and for the next two hours we caught up with his travel stories and his experiences in Buenos Aires. After a short rest, we walked around Ushuaia shopping centre and the ship docking area; then we went home for dinner which I prepared for the two boys. We had a restful evening and slept well.

16th March 2020

Robert, Alan and I woke up and thought a walk into town would be ideal; we also thought of trying a few of the tours offered in Ushuaia, while killing time for our Antarctica trip. We took breakfast and started the day by walking to the city centre to visit one of the tour companies. From the media it was apparent that coronavirus was taking a toll on some parts of the world, but the number of Argentinian infections was still quite low at that time. When we arrived at a certain local tour company they presented as if they were offering tours, but in fact they only offered transport to the start of the Laguna Esmeralda lake hike trail. Robert pulled the pin and decided to go back to the accommodation while Alan and I went ahead with our plan. (Alan was doubtful and wanted to pull out, but he agreed to go ahead anyway). We both paid and boarded the bus, but it did not leave immediately – we were kept waiting for quite a while and nobody communicated a word about anything. Once we started moving, the bus travelled for half an hour, then stopped and the driver indicated the start of the trail. It wasn't even a real trail; there was no proper demarcation of the route. Nevertheless, we took a gamble and undertook the walk to the lake. We were a group of five – an Argentinian couple, Alan, Matt (an Australian guy) and me. After one kilometre, Alan decided to go back and not to go ahead with the walk. It was a good decision, as he would not have made it through. Matt and I were in front as the Argentinian couple were taking their time walking.

My Australian co-walker confided in me that he had a poor sense of direction. For sure, he had no idea where we were going. I suggested that the only way to not get lost was to watch out for the well-worn trail where people had used the path. We went through forests, and then across wetlands where our shoes were completely covered with mud. We weren't sure what we were stepping on or how deep these wetlands were. After two hours of challenging walking, we got to the lake – a very pretty site but not worth the walk, to be honest. If I had known that, I would not have done it in the first place. Once at the lake we had no time to even rest, as it took us another two hours to undergo the same treacherous walk back, so that the bus would not leave without us. We only managed to take one or two photos before embarking on the walk again. After two hours I was happy to finish that part of the trip, and glad to see the bus was waiting for us, since we were in the middle of nowhere. I spotted a man who was selling cooked sausages from his car, so I spoilt myself with one; it made me feel so much better as up till then I had only had two pieces of fruit and some water, all the way to and from the lake.

The bus was not ready to leave until everyone was accounted for, but it was getting cold and I was scared my fingers were going to freeze since I get hypothermia very quickly. I put on my gloves and sat in the bus to warm up. The wait continued for more than an hour and then a group of three young men came and said they had lost their friends in the forest. They had no idea where they could have gone, since there was no phone or GPS coverage. Everybody in the bus understood those boys' predicament, and we were not in a hurry to leave until, hopefully, the two guys turned up. It was getting late and the driver decided to leave without the boys. Their three companions were begging him to wait, saying that they were happy to pay more money if the driver could hang on for a little longer so that they could see whether their friends would emerge from the thick forest. Their plea fell on deaf ears and the driver left the three boys, plus the lost ones, behind. To this day I'm not sure whether they managed to find their lost friends – or, even if they did find them, whether they managed to get back to Ushuaia from the middle of nowhere. Robert called me, as he was getting worried about my whereabouts. We had a chat and I reassured him I was going to be home soon, which I was, just before darkness fell.

Alan narrated how he had to wait for two more hours before the bus came to take him back to the city; he too had had a sausage on the side of the road. I had a cuppa as I told of my experiences for the day to both Robert and Alan. I washed my dirty boots, and then we went out for dinner. We wanted Alan to experience Bodegon Fueguino, the restaurant we had gone to two days ago, but the place was closed when we got there. We opted for pizza in a restaurant down the street; we ordered, but the service was not that great. The two pizzas we had ordered looked good but tasted ordinary. We only ate them because we were hungry and needed to fill our stomachs. Meanwhile, a lady approached our table and introduced herself as Sam; she said she heard us talk about going to Antarctica the following day. She informed us that all the cruise ships had stopped going as the government had banned all tourism activity and wanted all tourists out of Ushuaia within 24 hours. Sam was scheduled to visit Antarctica with a different cruise company, but her boat had more tourists than ours. We linked up with Sam on WhatsApp to enable us keep in touch and support each other where necessary. We had not heard back from our own cruise company, so we went back anxiously to our accommodation inn.

Confused and not sure where we were at, we sat on our bed contemplating what action we could take next. Just before we fell asleep, a message from Southern Antarctic Cruise came through on Robert's phone saying that all cruise tours had been cancelled, and they were urging us to look for flights to get out of Ushuaia as soon as possible. We also checked our email and saw that the company had written a generic letter saying that they were not refunding the cruise money, nor were they going to reschedule the tours in future. This trip had cost us a lot of money. To be told that your money would just disappear like that was devastating; we knew how much we had sacrificed to save it. Anyway, our priority at that point was to get flights out of Ushuaia as soon as we could. We could not sleep at all, as we tried to find tickets online without any success. Eventually we gave up and rested...

17th March 2020

We woke up early, and I went to Ushuaia airport; I left Robert and Alan behind as I could speak some Spanish and I thought it would be good for me to see whether I could secure our tickets. When I got to the airport there was a crowd of three hundred people there, all with their luggage; nobody was talking and there were no officials to address customers. I heard a couple talking and picked up that they were Australian, so I approached them to find out what was happening. They said they were in Antarctica but were recalled, since the Argentinian government had decided that foreigners had to leave immediately. They had been given no time to organise themselves. Their trip to Antarctica had been cut short and they were collected from the dock and driven straight to the airport. However, most flights were cancelled, particularly by the main airlines in Argentina. I left without talking to any official and without any tickets.

Back home, Robert and Alan were still browsing for tickets online. I joined them in browsing every site which offered flights out of Ushuaia. I also called every airline from Argentina, New Zealand and Australia but with no response; sometimes I waited on the phone for more than an hour before giving up. Robert and Alan went to the supermarket and bought food for a lovely lunch. I tried to enjoy the food even though I had no appetite. They both asked me to visit the supermarket and see for myself how people were organised. I went and saw people queuing outside; five people were allowed in at a time, in exchange for the ones coming out; no-one was allowed to buy in bulk. I was stunned at the level of organisation and patience; people were not being selfish. Everything else was closed; the place had suddenly become a ghost town.

It was morning in Australia, so I called our son Brian to try and follow up our tickets. After two hours on the phone he finally managed to secure tickets to Melbourne for us with Air New Zealand, leaving on the 20th March. I'm not sure how we can ever reward our children, as both Brian and Alexandria worked really hard to ensure we were both safe and not stressing out. I also managed to secure local tickets from Ushuaia to Buenos Aires. Although all our tickets were ready to go, securing accommodation in Buenos Aires was a nightmare as hotels were getting rid of tourists and not accommodating anyone. We got in touch with Australian Consular officials who provided us with an accommodation option which took tourists on the condition that they had to be quarantined. We were all set to leave Argentina well before things went from bad to worse. MaryAnne, Alan's wife, booked his ticket from Australia and he was set to leave after us.

Homeward Bound:

18th March 2020

Our flight from Ushuaia to Buenos Aires with LATAM Airlines (based in Chile) was smooth, with not too many passengers. We arrived at Jorge Newbery airport in Greater Buenos Aires, and while collecting our bags met some more Australians who had been through the same experience as ourselves. One of the couples came from Robert's hometown in South Gippsland – what a small world! However, they were leaving Argentina that night and only needed to kill time awaiting their flight. Another guy, Pete, joined us; he was staying in Argentina till the 23rd, so we thought since we were going to be quarantined in the hotel, we would take some time to have coffee and food. We killed three hours here in the company of a few Australians. The couple took a taxi straight to Ezeiza airport, while Pete shared a taxi with us, and we were dropped first at the door of our accommodation. Pete continued in the taxi; we did not get his contact details, so we never found out how he got on.

    The supermarket was just around the corner so we ventured in to buy our groceries for our stay in the hotel. Robert did the shopping while I watched over the luggage at the entrance. The government had announced limitations on people's movements and therefore there were very few people on the street; if you were a foreigner, people looked at you in a weird manner. While Robert was in the supermarket, the air conditioner broke and fell from the roof; it missed him by a whisker but he got bruised on the right eye. He was lucky it did not hit him directly, otherwise it could have been another story. We were also told we could only use uber eats or get charged for groceries; the situation was not very tourist-friendly.

It was 4.00 pm and our time to go to the hotel was nearing. Just the thought of being isolated in a hotel room was killing me internally but there was nothing I could do. To delay the moment, we called Nesa to see whether she wanted to come over and spent some time with us at the park, since she was staying near our hotel. She was happy to come around and we sat down in a park next to the hotel waiting for her. Once she arrived, she was very emotional and happy to see us; she had become like a daughter and required a lot of reassurance. Nesa had a ticket to her home in Switzerland for the 21st March; she was upset that she was not going to visit Australia, but it was critical at this point to be safe and get home to her parents. Another two hours disappeared just like that, chatting to Nesa, before darkness fell, and we went off to our hotel and into isolation. We checked into our room on the seventh floor; we had a small kitchenette, a bathroom and a small balcony.

19th March 2020

We were sleeping well on our first night, but just after 2.00 am Alan called and said to check our ticket, as Air New Zealand had suspended all flights without any notice. I was still sleepy and thought it was a bad dream. Panic kicked in, and immediately I was on the internet trying to find out what was happening. We checked our emails but there was nothing from Air New Zealand, but the news was everywhere on the media. Our difficulties in leaving Argentina had begun. Just as we thought we were all set for a smooth trip back home, it appeared this was not going to happen. The race to get another ticket to Australia started on the internet, but nothing was forthcoming. I got on the phone to Brian to see whether he could secure a ticket for us from Australia, with no luck either. Finally, we got a ticket from Qantas flying from Argentina, stopping in Auckland, New Zealand, and then on to Melbourne. The ticket cost 8,000 dollars for both of us and was scheduled for the 23rd March. While on Facebook we saw that 'Chimu Adventures' were organising charter flights from both Argentina and Peru to get Australians out of those two countries. Therefore, we joined the group and paid another ten thousand dollars as our backup. Our main aim was to survive the four days before our flight was due. But I was so uneasy not knowing what the Argentinian government was going to do next, and also with the fear of being stuck in a hotel and not being able to go back home.

20th March 2020

Meanwhile, I got in touch with Sam early in the morning to see how she was doing, and she panicked, checked out of her hotel and headed to the airport. She was lucky enough to get her ticket changed, and she got to fly out that morning to Santiago then direct to Melbourne. In the morning, I told Robert we should go to the airport and try our luck, even though our ticket was scheduled for the 23rd March. After a bit of argument, he reluctantly agreed to go with me. So, we packed everything and talked to the hotel management about allowing us back if it all backfired in terms of getting flights. We arrived at the airport well before 7 am and queued, although there were very few people at the airport. We spoke to a lady who told us that our Qantas ticket was a big problem. Why? The New Zealand government would not allow any Australian plane on their soil or in their air space. Our problems started from there. She said we had no option other than buy another ticket. Well, we were not looking to buy another ticket, but what choice did we have? The Argentinian government did not want any foreigners on its soil, the atmosphere on the ground was not very welcoming and we did not want to be holed up in a hotel not knowing when we could get out of the country. The ticket lady referred us to another counter where we were supposed to purchase yet another ticket.

The lady on this counter possessed customer relations skills, and we explained that we had been advised to buy yet another ticket to Australia. After spending some time on the computer, she said all the flights were full and the only option was on the 26th March, which was too far away as things were changing every two minutes. We were not sure whether the Argentinian government was going to lock down everything the following day. All we wanted was to get out, and here we were with no options available. I decided to explain that we had a ticket already for Australia, but we were told we could not use it since we were transiting through New Zealand. She decided to have a look at our ticket, then she was on the computer for ten minutes and she finally got us a flight to leave Buenos Aires the following day, 21st March. One more day was not going to kill us, so we went back to our hotel and tried to rest for the remainder of the day. We ate and slept, waiting for the new dawn and to see whether we could leave Argentina.

21st March 2020

I woke early in the morning and checked on the flight tracking apps. There were three flights scheduled for that day, but I was not confident of the facts on the internet. The situation was changing from one minute to the next. I prepared breakfast at 4.00am, keen to leave, although it was too early. I woke Robert up for breakfast and we had a discussion on the importance of going to the airport early, so that if one flight cancelled, we would have an opportunity to catch another one. We agreed to go to the airport at 6.30 am. There was a flight scheduled for 8.30 am, and we got there well on time, but it was cancelled. Our flight was scheduled for 11.28 am for Santiago in Chile, so we still had a chance to fly if it was going to happen. We waited in anxious anticipation, and the time to fly came. We went through the security check but just before Robert got his screening done, he realised he had misplaced his boarding pass. What a drama! He spent another five minutes going through all his belongings, checking where on earth he could have put his boarding pass. I suggested that maybe he put it in his top shirt pocket. Sure enough, that is where it was. I was almost having a heart attack thinking we were so close to boarding the aeroplane only to lose the flight through a misplaced boarding pass.

We boarded the plane; two more passengers came on board, then we waited for another twenty minutes. No more passengers entered on the plane. Never in my whole life have I flown in an empty aircraft. This was the first time we had had a private jet to ourselves. There were four cabin crew members and they could not trace where the other customers were, so we seated ourselves where we chose. It was weird to see a whole aeroplane empty except for four passengers. The crew members were great, and we received a snack and a drink. The view as we flew over the Andes was wonderful, and we landed in Santiago ready to for our last leg to Australia.

22nd March 2020: Santiago, Chile

Santiago International Airport in Chile is such a big place, but there were no signs as to where we were supposed to go, nor anybody to talk to. Along with the other two passengers from our plane, we walked along a high roofed corridor following the exit and the connecting flight sign. Finally, we got to the duty-free shops and the lounge where other passengers were waiting. Our plane to Australia was scheduled to leave at 2.00 am, so we went straight to the desk of LATAM airlines (which works in collaboration with Qantas) to try and make sure that the flight was still on. We were prepared for a full day hanging around the airport. After, we presented our tickets, the lady behind the counter said she was sorry, but our scheduled flight was cancelled. We were dumbstruck. We had not planned for this continuing drama with our ticket! We thought that this issue had already been sorted out, but we were so wrong – the problems had just begun again. Automatically, one thinks that the airline would put one on the next flight to Australia, but . . . no. Now a fight started between LATAM and Qantas. LATAM airline informed us that our next flight would be with them the following day at 02.00 hours. However, there was also a Qantas flight leaving at 13.00 hours the following day. It did not make sense to me to wait for LATAM since our ticket had been bought directly from Qantas.

One hour went by as we waited for LATAM to sort us out, but there was no definite answer as to whether we were going to travel. It seemed like we had tickets, but they were not recognised, and time was running out as all the flights were finishing on the 25th March – perhaps, because things were changing by the hour. Next, LATAM airline informed me that their system was down! It took two hours for it to re-surface. Well, at the end of those two hours I was at the same counter and same messages were being passed on to me. At one point I was getting so frustrated as nothing seemed to work that I called Brian in Australia and asked him to visit the Qantas desk and see what was happening with our tickets, since we were completely lost and nobody was taking any responsibility. Brian got in touch with us after two hours and said Robert could fly with Qantas, but they could not even trace me on the system. How crazy was that? The tickets had been bought using a single credit card and as a package, not as individual tickets. There was nothing much the Qantas office could do, apparently, and our situation remained the same. LATAM kept telling me to visit their counter every two hours.

Two days spent on Santiago airport seats are not the most comfortable experience one might imagine having. However, we had no choice. We continued nagging LATAM staff to fix our ticket, and at one point they said we had to purchase another. I had no idea why the tickets could not be honoured, and it was difficult to purchase a new one. All our energy and adrenaline were gone, and our anxiety levels were going up, even though we had each other to rely on, and boosted one another's morale. The miracle was, after all this, that we were still married, and this experience had not called for a divorce! Finally, I had enough of being tossed from one airline to another and I put my foot down. I told LATAM to transfer us to Qantas since we had purchased our tickets from them. The lady must have had enough of me. She printed a paper for me to present to a Qantas official whenever they arrived to check people in at their counter. Robert had not an ounce of energy left and the fear of not being able to fly out of Santiago was wearing him down. But he presented himself at the Qantas counter two hours before the check-in staff arrived for work, and he was first in the queue to be attended to.

Meanwhile, we had met some more Australians either waiting to sort out their tickets (as LATAM had messed them up too) or to change from a later date to an earlier one. It was somewhat comforting to know that we were not the only ones facing this issue with the tickets; however, we could only hope the issue would be sorted out once and for all by Qantas officials. Time was moving very slowly, and nobody knew when the Qantas counter was going to open; we had three suggested opening times, ranging from 9.00 to 11.00 am. When the officials finally arrived, everyone clapped their hands as a sign of relief! The two officials showed no emotion or recognition of our plight. Robert, the first in the queue, presented his printed paper from LATAM. I was standing next to him but keeping quiet. I did not know what else I could do; we both felt so vulnerable. The lady glanced at the paper and said we were flying with LATAM; I protested and opened my phone, showing her that I purchased the ticket with Qantas. We did not know why LATAM were even involved, except for the flight from Buenos Aires. Qantas business with LATAM is between the two of them but it should not interfere with the required services to customers.

After the Qantas lady looked at my ticket, she put

the reference number through her computer and said she could not find us on the system. I asked her whether the plane was full and she firmly said no – so we had a little bit of hope that if it wasn't full, we might have a chance of purchasing another ticket if the one we had was not validated. She took a photo of our ticket and said she was communicating with her supervisor to try and fix it. But we had to stand aside and wait for her response. Two hours later, she finished checking everyone in, and then came back to us. There were around five of us in total with issues, and she started sorting us out one by one. Every time she ran my passport, she could not read it on the computer since I was still not on the system. We were getting extremely nervous. Finally, she confirmed that her supervisor had fixed everything, and she could process our boarding passes. Time was running out before departure and we were the last ones to board the aeroplane. We ran all the way to Gate 9, not wanting the plane to leave without us. We left our bags behind as there was no time to get them transferred. At this stage we did not care about bags. All we wanted was to land in Australia; it didn't matter where in Australia, provided we were on Australian soil. We found the aeroplane just boarding and talked to some of the people who had met us earlier, who were happy to see us all going home. The plane left at 13.00 and before it even left the ground everyone was clapping, a sign that they were happy to leave Santiago.

We landed in Sydney at 18.00 hours on Monday evening to a very quiet airport. Everyone, including Robert and myself, was so happy to land at home. We had teary eyes reflecting on all that we had gone through, and the experience this Corona virus had brought into our lives. There was no way we could have predicted that the world would have changed so quickly and dramatically; nor that individual governments would make decisions which they thought fitted their citizens, but which left outsiders stranded. The concept of globalisation went out of the window during this Corona virus pandemic, and the world retreated back to an existence as individual nations. Anyway, our main aim after our arrival was to see whether we could follow up our luggage. There was no queue, for once, at the luggage counter, so we were served promptly and allocated a number. After which we took a bus to the domestic terminal. On arrival we presented our disputed ticket to the Qantas counter to see whether we could secure our ticket to Melbourne since our original ticket had been purchased for Melbourne. The lady behind the counter was more than helpful, did not have any issues finding us on their system. She called her supervisor and in no time, we had our tickets to Melbourne.

We arrived in Melbourne at 22.00 hours, got home, and the children had set us up in the garage to commence our fourteen days of quarantine. It was hard not to be able to cuddle our children; all we could do was wave at each other from a distance. We settled for a good night's sleep, knowing for sure we were home. We obtained the luggage ticket and waited to see whether Qantas were going to trace it and deliver it home.

Self-Quarantine At Home

23rd March 2020

We normally use our garage to store all the junk we do not need every day, such as garden tools, old books and cartons. However, there is a little bit of space where the kids had improvised a bed from a mattress and linen for our use, and created a place to cook. We had an outside toilet, and Robert even built an outside makeshift shower room. This experience was a good way of getting back to the basics of life, and realising that one does not need a lot of material things to survive in this world. The concept of moving around in a limited space was not appealing; however, I was at home and not stuck in a hotel room. I thought of it as a version of going camping, but this time in our own backyard. Our Day One was exciting as we spent the time organising and putting things in different locations to make the space comfortable for our stay. We wanted to isolate properly as it would be horrible to pass the virus on to our loved ones if we did have it, and it was also the right thing to do. We also have a small garden and even though we were in quarantine we could spend a bit of time doing gardening. I could water my flowers and Robert could look after his herbs – while completing the bathroom.

The feeling of waking up in our own home was the best thing ever! We slept in. Jet lag had taken its toll, so we needed time to relax and get back into a normal routine. Robert made a cup of tea, brought it next to the bed and put it on the floor – since we had no side table. That morning we got in touch with family members and friends who had been with us throughout this journey. The afternoon went by without arguments or disagreements. I suppose if one can manage to stay in quarantine in a Buenos Aires hotel one can survive anywhere! Luckily, we have learnt to appreciate each other's company.

The temporary bathroom was finished, so I gave it a go. Even though it had been made with love, I only used it when it was sunny – because the top was open and it was very cold when the sun was not up! However, I used the outside toilet to 'shower' at times by putting a bucket on top of the toilet, with a container underneath to collect the water. I used both the outside bathroom when it was sunny, and other times I used the toilet and enjoyed my showers immensely. The only thing I found difficult was washing my hair in this set up; however, I managed to work that out eventually.

We used a whiteboard located in front of the door to communicate what we wanted for our daily living, and to send shopping lists so the children could get things from the supermarket for us. We did our own cooking and exercised daily to keep healthy. It was day six at this time, we had eight more days left and we never underestimated the importance of movement.

1st April 2020

We were still in quarantine. I never realised how long two weeks could be, particularly if one was doing nothing much with one's life. I embarked on writing my stories, which I dedicated, time to each afternoon. The mornings were spent watching the depressing news about COVID-19, then stepping out into the garden in the sun; I put a bean bag on the ground and just sat enjoying the fresh air. When the kids came out from the house they would sit at a distance from where we were within the garden and were happy to chat about anything. If nothing else, this quarantine was making some families get closer – even though some family members were suffering from the restrictions and isolation.

My best friend Susan is based in Finland. We have been friends for a very long time; with the internet it's as if we are just around the corner from one another. She wrote me a moving happy birthday message, but she sent it on the wrong date. I pointed out I was glad to receive the message and it made me teary, but she had the wrong date. She responded by saying of course she did know my date of birth, but that the corona virus must have made her a bit crazy. Well, it turned out she wasn't not the only one mistaking the date, because another close friend named Anne in East Gippsland also sent a bouquet of flowers the same day. Actually, I was glad to get them a day early.

Anyway, I also took time to call various airlines for flight refunds and the waiting time on the telephones was atrocious – from one to two hours of being on hold! I managed to process three airlines the day I started, and was hoping I would be able to get through all of them by the end of the week. After contacting Air New Zealand and putting our case forward they were negotiating, offering to provide a voucher for us to use whenever we travelled again. We preferred to have our money refunded and I was not going to take a no for an answer. I declined their voucher offer. After a few minutes on the phone they agreed to refund our ticket. Within two days the money was in our account, and even though they initially treated us badly they were quick to process the full ticket refund, which was very much appreciated. We also managed to get a refund from Chimu Adventures – one of their conditions had been to get in touch with them early enough if we couldn't travel, so they had time to get more people to fill the aircraft. We acted promptly as soon as we managed to fly out from Argentina and as promised they kept their side of the bargain.

Around midday Qantas staff called to inform us that our luggage had been found and was to be dropped at home. True to their word, that evening we had our bags. What a prompt service which we never expected!

We did not feel like cooking after a day of phoning and negotiating, so we asked Brian to get fish and chips. I do not normally eat junk foods and take-away, but I must say I did enjoy those chips. We slept well waiting for my birthday to come the next day.

The Great Birthday!

2nd April 2020

My mother told me that when I was born it rained the whole night. Well, turning fifty there was no difference – it rained the whole day and night. I could hear the rain pounding the roof of the garage and thought what a great time to be born. Morning came and Robert wished me a happy birthday. All he could offer was a cup of tea in bed. There was nothing much we could do on my birthday as being in quarantine restricted us from even going out together. Australia had also restricted the movement of people, and restaurants were not operating, so even if we had been able to go out there would have been nowhere to go.

We were healthy and although our idea had been to escape to South America to have my fiftieth birthday celebration there, circumstances forced us to return to where we belonged and have a celebration at home. The weather that day was gloomy with grey clouds, but otherwise we enjoyed what life had to provide. Just before we organised our day, Brian called us out and said that the police had arrived to check whether we were doing the right thing in quarantine, and wanted to talk to us. We invited them to come around to the garage, and they needed to see our passports. I had mine in the garage while Robert's was in the main house. They were not fussy about it, had a look at mine, ticked it off their register, then settled in for a chat. For the next fifteen minutes we chatted with the police officers about our corona virus adventures, including some of our travel experiences. They were pleasant and happy to chat, and pleased we were doing the right thing.

My birthday afternoon was nothing special although in the evening the children gave me a surprise, just when I thought we were settling in to watching corona virus news. Alexandria called me outside and she surprised me with some flowers, champagne, a birthday card and a candle in the dark. It was a lovely treat and I could not have asked for anything more. After singing 'happy birthday', we retreated to the garage and had a good night. The remaining days were spent doing nothing much. The novelty of being in quarantine had worn off and all I wanted was to feel free! I knew the rest of the country was restricted and locked down, but in my brain, I yearned for that feeling of freedom.

6th-7th April 2020

Finally, our last day of quarantine and sleeping in the garage arrived. I was both excited and sad, at the same time. Just before the day ended a couple of police officers visited again. I thought Alexandria was pulling my leg when she said the police were at the front door of the house. I wondered why they had come twice, as we thought we had 'passed the test' by complying with the quarantine protocol. They came around to the garage and announced that they wanted to see Robert's passport. Robert was enjoying his shower in his makeshift bathroom and could not come out, so instead they asked for his driver's licence, which I provided, then they signed off their register. I did tell them that two other policemen had come two days ago, which left them lost for words. Anyway, they left without any drama.

After watching the news, I went to bed early and slept very well. Robert seemed to have developed a routine of being settled into the new environment and did not seem excited at being able to go back to the main house, have a nice warm shower and feel free at last. He mentioned that he was happy to continue using the garage more often after this experience. I slept in but woke up feeling terrible – I did not have any of the symptoms associated with coronavirus but my body felt lethargic. I was so worried that after fourteen days in isolation, I might have contracted the virus – and so worried that I might have passed it to my daughter, who had come to the garage first thing in the morning after we completed quarantine. Alexandria was missing us, and she had come to the garage early in the morning to tell me that she had put the kettle on for a cup of tea. I was excited to leave the garage but not sure what I was going to do with all the time on my hands. I decided to clean up the garage, put things back to their normal places, and then went to the main house.

Finally, I was back in the main house. I took a nice shower, washed my hair and felt lovely and fresh. I also embarked on cleaning the house. It wasn't that it was dirty; it just felt like the right thing to do. We had a lamb leg in the freezer, and I wanted so much to have a nice roasted lamb with vegetables! Unfortunately, we could not defrost it in time to cook it. I cooked something else for dinner, and for the first time in four weeks we sat down as a family and enjoyed a meal together. We all so appreciated being there as a family.

8th April 2020

What a wonderful feeling waking up in our own bed and enjoying the little things we had missed. I still felt terribly lethargic, but had no symptoms that would justify a visit to the doctor. Even so, I decided that if I was feeling the same tomorrow, I would visit the general practitioner. I played it cool and observed myself, even though I was confused as to why I felt terrible now, even though during the previous fourteen days I had felt perfectly well. The day went by without much ado. Finally, evening came, and Robert made his special roast – of all our family he is the best at that – and we all enjoyed the food. Robert is lucky in that he can work from home, and yes, the garage has become his office and he seems content with the whole set up. We slept well having experienced freedom, even though the things we could do were limited. The following day, I felt perfectly well and back to being myself, so I let the family know that I did not feel sick any more. I knew that boredom and 'doing nothing much' was the next thing that was going to take a toll on my life. I am used to working long hours, but now that almost everything has come to a halt, I can only become creative, and go for walks. Hopefully, days will pass and soon life to go back to more like normal – if what we know as normality will ever return. Only time will tell.

Reflecting back on our trip, we felt that we had been perfectly organised to achieve the dream of our life time. Nothing untoward seemed to be on the way until the unprecedented COVID–19 came into existence. The fear and desperation associated with the virus and individual countries looking after their own was a good reminder that globalisation is great when everything is working perfectly well and everyone can benefit from it. However, the unusual timing of this unknown disease left tourists feeling unwanted. Even though there was a lot of uncertainty we never regretted our travels; we acquired other skills and experiences we could not have gained in our lifetime. We learnt that no matter where one travels, money plays a big factor and one cannot afford not to have some extra cash just in case plans are dismantled. As we discovered, it is important to have tours and trips booked well in advance. However, that way you also run the risk of losing all your money, since organisations and tour companies are happy to renege on their own policies. Travel insurance policies are not very reliable, either, when it comes to compensation, as they claim to never cover pandemics, even when the policy was paid well before any such pandemic existed. Lastly the use of third parties for bookings can be a high risk, even though at times there is no choice. After negotiation with the cruise company they accepted to defer our tour to 2021 or 2022 depending on the opening of international borders. No refunds, however. So, our dream is not yet dead and hopefully when COVID–19 is well under control we shall embark on another trip to Antarctica. Dreams never die, and having hope keeps the fire alive!

Jane N. Hughes

Floralia Generica, Buenos Aires

Our empty plane, Buenos Aires

Our rough walk to Laguna Esmeralda, Ushuaia

Laguna Esmeralda, Ushuaia

Jane N. Hughes

On the way to Martial Glacier, Ushuaia

A closer look at martial glacier, Ushuaia

Jane N. Hughes

Posing at Ushuaia

Jane N. Hughes

Acknowledgments

The production of a book, however small, involves much more than one's own writing. I am grateful for family support from my husband Robert for his moral support, motivation and encouragement during our trip, enabling me to pull through during what were often trying times. Our children Brian and Alexandria for continued support, both when we were away and when we got back home, and my brother Moses, for keeping me positive with his sense of humour throughout the adventure.

I am also indebted to a trusted and valued circle of friends who encouraged putting my stories into a book. My long term friend Anne for reading my first manuscript and providing valuable commentary. Richard for his continued comments, opinions, guidance and time. And lastly to my best friend Susan who, even though based in Finland she was always there for me and providing sisterly support finally, I am grateful